390

D1716766

WHALES

WHALES

BY HELEN HOKE
AND VALERIE PITT

DRAWINGS BY
THOMAS R. FUNDERBURK

FRANKLIN WATTS, INC.
NEW YORK · 1973

←A FIRST BOOK→

The authors and publisher would like to thank the following experts for their helpful suggestions: Steve Leatherwood, Director, Whale Watch, Department of the Navy; Frederick P. Schmitt, Curator, Whaling Museum Society; and Richard C. Whaley, Chesapeake Bay Institute, The Johns Hopkins University.

Picture credits: Steve Leatherwood, Whale Watch Program, Department of the Navy: pages 12, 27, 39 (top and bottom), 76 (bottom); Marineland of the Pacific, 17, 23, 52 (top and bottom), 56 (top), 63, 64; Miami Seaquarium: 19, 56 (bottom); The New York Public Library Picture Collection: 69 (top and bottom); Sea World, Inc.: 60 (top); Smithsonian Institution: 32; U.S. Information Agency: 76 (top); U.S. Navy: 28, 60 (bottom).

Cover design by Al Pisano

Library of Congress Cataloging in Publication Data

Hoke, Helen, 1903-
    Whales.

    (A First book)
    SUMMARY: Describes the characteristics and habits which all whales have in common and the distinctive features of the different kinds of whales, including dolphins and porpoises.
    Bibliography: p.
    1. Whales – Juvenile literature. [1. Whales. 2. Dolphins. 3. Porpoises] I. Pitt, Valerie, joint author. II. Title.
QL737.C4H64   599'.5   72-11769
ISBN 0-531-00779-0

CONTENTS

LARGER THAN
THE DINOSAURS

If you have ever seen a whale, you will understand why these animals have been treated with awe and respect since the earliest times. Some whales are enormous, the most enormous creatures that have ever inhabited the earth — bigger even than the largest known dinosaurs.

The giant of the family is the blue whale, which may measure 90 feet or more in length and may weigh an astounding 150 tons (300,000 pounds) — more than the combined weight of 2,000 people. It is the largest animal the world has known — big enough to fill an average-sized house from front to back. One blue whale was even more colossal. It measured 113 feet in length and weighed an estimated 170 tons — a record.

Even the very smallest members of the whale family, some of the porpoises, grow to 5 feet in length.

Along with their cousins the dolphins and the porpoises, whales belong to the scientific order *Cetacea* (*see*-TAY-shee-a). Collectively they are known as Cetaceans. They inhabit all the seas and oceans and some rivers of the world, but a great many of them live in the coldest regions — the ice-lashed seas of the Arctic and the Antarctic.

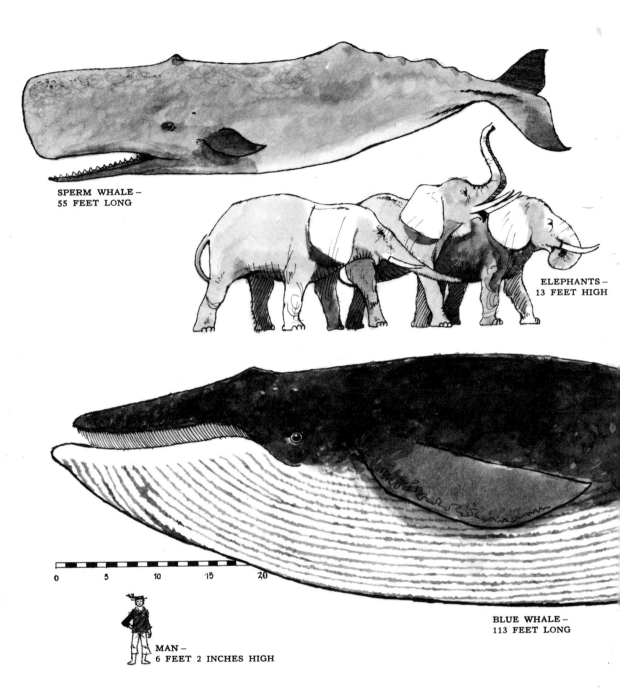

SPERM WHALE –
55 FEET LONG

ELEPHANTS –
13 FEET HIGH

0   5   10   15   20

BLUE WHALE –
113 FEET LONG

MAN –
6 FEET 2 INCHES HIGH

DOLPHINS —
10 FEET LONG

DINOSAUR —
55 FEET LONG

KILLER WHALE —
28 FEET LONG

75   80   85   90   100   105

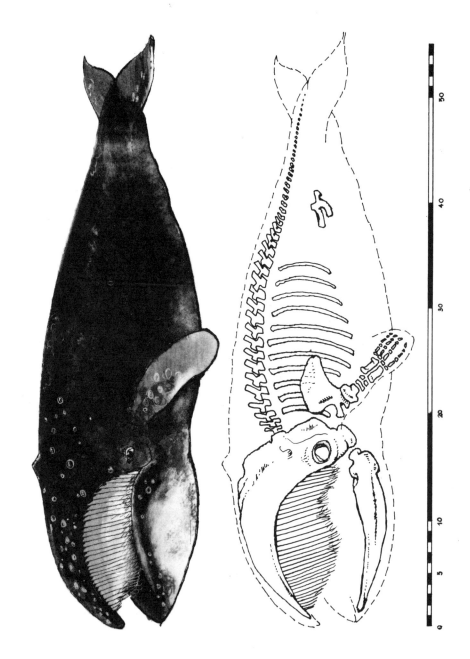

Although we do not know who their direct ancestors were, although scientists suspect they are descended from insectivore-creodont (rodent-like mammals) stock, we do know that the forerunners of whales once made their home on land. Even now, inside their bodies, whales have traces of bones that show that they once must have had four legs. They have small bones that look almost like hands inside their flippers. And some have small hipbones, which are probably all that remain of hind legs. None of these bones is needed by sea creatures, but they would have been important to animals who lived on land and walked about there. These bones are clues to the long-ago life of the whales.

We also do not know why whales left the land and took to the sea, but the water's rich food supply was probably an important attraction. And with bountiful food supplies, the whale grew and grew and grew. Because water can support great weight, if the weight is evenly distributed, there was nothing to limit a whale's size.

Now, of course, whales live entirely in the water and never go ashore. If by accident a whale is stranded on a beach, it suffocates. Without the buoyancy of the water to keep it afloat, and because of the pull of gravity on land, the whale's enormous bulk pushes down so hard that its lungs and other organs collapse. Without its lungs the whale cannot breathe and it dies; death is often hastened by overexposure.

Greenland right whale
and its skeleton (simplified)

SHAPED LIKE
A FISH,
BUT NOT A FISH

Although it is a sea creature and looks somewhat like a huge fish, the whale is actually not a fish at all. Like its land ancestors, it is a mammal.

All mammals have four main characteristics in common:
- They all have lungs and breathe air.
- They are warm-blooded, with body temperatures that remain constant. The whale's temperature is about 96.8°, close to man's, and it remains the same, whatever the outside temperature.
- All mammals have some hair; although the whale is generally a smooth creature, it does have a few whiskery hairs on its chin or head.
- Mammals give birth to live young, which they nurse with milk.

Nearly all mammals live on land. Man is a mammal. So are tigers and elephants and chimpanzees and cats and dogs. A mammal's characteristics make it highly suited to life on land where there is air to breathe; sunshine and clothes or fur for keeping warm; a great variety of foods; and suitable places for giving birth to young.

How then does the whale manage to live the life of a mammal in the ocean? The answer is that it has become adapted, or fitted, to an ocean life. Take its shape, for instance. A human cannot move easily through water. For one thing, his legs are too heavy. Normally they must carry his whole body about on land and work against the pull of gravity. In water, a human's strong legs will eventually cause him to sink. And besides, the angles of his body — his narrow limbs and unwebbed, spreading fingers and toes — are too awkward and numerous to cope with resistant water pressure. For easy traveling in the sea an animal needs a streamlined shape and evenly distributed weight.

Whales have been called "efficient living submarines." Their huge heads and bodies merge into a continuous smooth torpedo shape that offers little resistance to water pressure. The head, which may measure a third of the whale's entire body, is supported by neckbones which, in many whales, are fused together so that the animal cannot turn its head from side to side. The front limbs have become smooth flippers, which the whale uses for balancing, steering, and braking. They can be rotated, which adds to their usefulness when the whale needs to change direction. Some whales have a second balancing and steering device called a dorsal fin, along their backs, near their tails. The tail itself is horizontally spread out and ends in two large flukes, or lobes. (A fish's tail is vertical and moves from side to side.)

The whale's flukes drive it through the water. Composed of tough, flexible tissue, they are powered by strong muscles. As the horizontal tail goes up and down each fluke moves in turn in opposite cycles, twisting through the water with powerful strokes. So strong are the flukes that one lash from them may smash a small boat in two. They propel the whale at speeds which, for short bursts, may reach 18 knots (about 21 miles)

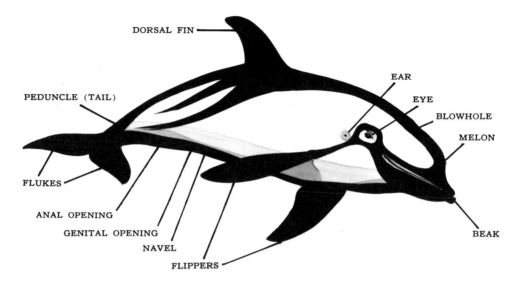

DORSAL FIN

EAR

EYE

BLOWHOLE

MELON

PEDUNCLE (TAIL)

FLUKES

ANAL OPENING

GENITAL OPENING

NAVEL

FLIPPERS

BEAK

The anatomy of a Cetacean

*The head and body of a Cetacean
(little piked whale) merge into
a torpedo shape, offering little
resistance to water pressure.*

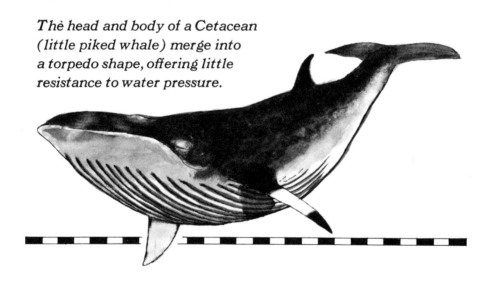

an hour, or more if the whale is frightened. The fin whale can maintain a speed of 20 knots for fifteen minutes or more, and the dolphins can go even faster — up to 25 knots.

Land mammals usually have hair or a coat of fur to keep their body warmth from dissipating into the surrounding air, but thick hair would slow down the whale. It needs smooth skin for sliding through the water.

To keep warm, whales, and other sea mammals like seals and walruses, have a layer of blubber just under their thin outer skin. Blubber, which is tissue rich in fat and oil, acts as an insulating wall against the chilly water. In porpoises, the layer is only about an inch thick, but it may be more than a foot thick in the largest whales. The whale's streamlined shape also helps keep it warm. With no angles and with only small flippers, the body has less surface exposed to the cold water

Flukes of a killer whale,
fin whale, humpback, and sperm whale

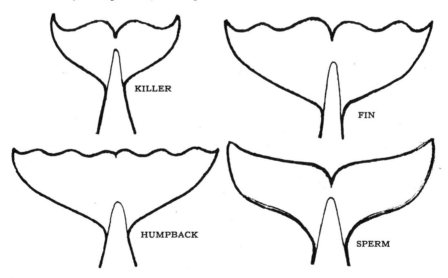

KILLER

FIN

HUMPBACK

SPERM

than most mammals would. It is on surface layers that heat is given up to the water.

During long voyages to feeding grounds, whales often do not stop to eat, but draw nourishment from their blubber in much the same way that bears and woodchucks live on their body fat during hibernation. By the time whales arrive at their winter homes, the blubber may have become very thin.

But what happens when a whale gets too hot? In tropical seas, it cannot get rid of body heat by sweating or panting as land mammals do. When a whale gets too hot, blood vessels in the blubber bring the excess heat close to the whale's thin skin, which is cooled by the surrounding water. The whale's body heat is also regulated by alterations in the blood flow through the flippers and the flukes.

All mammals have to breathe air to live. The whale is no exception. But breathing air is a far more complicated matter for whales than for most other mammals, for whales find their food in the sea, either near the surface or deep below it, where breathing is impossible. Every time the whale dives beneath the sea's surface, it must hold its breath.

The maximum time a professional human diver can hold his breath is two and a half minutes. Whales may dive for longer periods. The sperm whale can stay submerged for an hour or more.

How does the whale hold its breath for such a long time? Once again, the whale has adapted to life in the water. In other mammals the nostrils are placed at the front of the face. But the whale has nostrils on top of its head. Some whales have one nostril (called a blowhole); others have two. Because whales always surface headfirst, they can get air through the blowhole quickly.

A fin whale's powerful flukes drive it through the water (tail movement exaggerated).

The open twin blowholes of a blue whale. Baleen whales
have paired blowholes, toothed whales have only one.

Before a dive, the whale takes an enormous breath through the blowhole. The nostrils bypass the mouth and connect directly to the lungs, so that the whale can open its mouth underwater to get food. As the whale submerges, flaps close over the blowhole so that no water can enter the lungs. The whale can hold its breath for a long time because as it dives deep into the water its blood circulation changes drastically. The heartbeat slows down. A slower beat makes the blood itself move more slowly. Ordinarily, blood carries oxygen to every part of the body, but when the whale dives, muscles stop the flow of blood to all the organs except the heart, lungs, and brain. They must have oxygen if the whale is to survive. The rest of the whale's organs and tissues can go for several hours without constantly receiving oxygen.

A human diver who goes deep down into the ocean must wear a special diving suit and have air pumped down to him through an air hose. The air is under high pressure. The deeper the diver goes, the more the air pressure increases. Air contains not only oxygen gas but also nitrogen gas. Under heavy air pressure the nitrogen dissolves in the diver's blood. If he comes up too quickly, the change from high-pressure air to lower-pressure air happens so fast that the nitrogen changes to gas bubbles in his blood. The bubbles press on the body tissues and block up blood vessels, causing a painful and dangerous condition known as the bends. To avoid the bends, the diver must come back to the surface slowly, stopping altogether at times so that the air decompresses gradually.

Some whales dive to astounding depths to find food. The sperm whale is probably the champion diver. One sperm whale was found entangled in an underwater cable more than 3,000 feet deep in the Pacific Ocean. In other species, dives of several hundred feet are more usual.

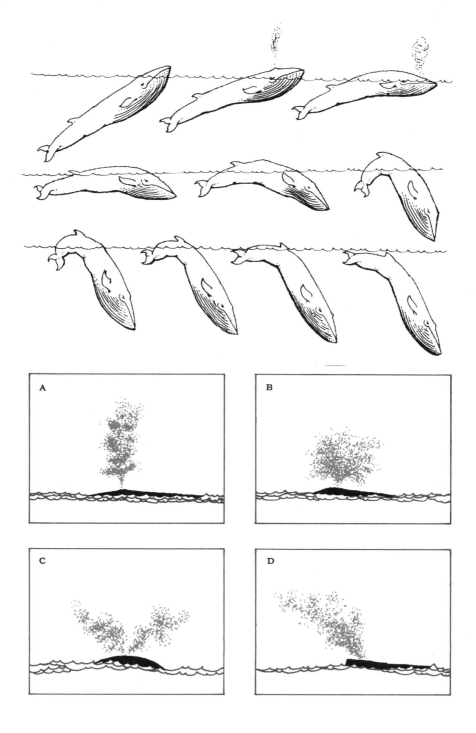

Despite these deep dives, whales do not get the bends. Why not? The reason seems to be quite simple. Whales never take in a dangerous amount of nitrogen in the first place. Unlike the human diver, who is constantly receiving air through his air hose, the whale takes in only one great lungful of air at the beginning of his dive. That lungful contains only a normal amount of nitrogen.

When the whale finally resurfaces, all the air he has held in his lungs is forced out through the blowhole in a great stream. This action is known as blowing, or spouting. The air, a gas, has been warmed by the whale's body, and when it hits the cooler, outside air it condenses and changes to vapor. Like a cloud floating on top of the water, the steamy spout may climb 20 feet into the sky and may be seen from a mile away. Lookouts on old whaling ships, upon seeing a spout, shouted the old whaling cry, "Blows! Ah, blows!" Experienced whalers can often tell the type of whale from the kind of spout it shoots into the air. It may be V-shaped or cone-shaped, tall and slender, or short and fuzzily outlined.

After the whale has surfaced, it takes a long series of rapid breaths to put oxygen back into its bloodstream and tissues.

How do whales sleep in the water? Like some other mammals, most whales take short naps night or day, whenever they feel the need of them, although the sperm whale is reported to be a deep sleeper. Whales sleep on the surface of the water with their blowholes above the surface. Several kinds of toothed whales have been seen to nap with their eyes shut.

Above, the sequence of a fin whale surfacing, spouting, and sounding. Below, the spouts of a baleen whale (A) and humpback (B); the double spout of a right whale (C) and the forward slanting spout of the sperm (D).

UNDERWATER BIRTH

Unlike birds or most fish and reptiles, who lay eggs, mammals give birth to live young. The fetus — the baby animal in its early stages of growth — develops inside the mother's body and is not born until it is fully formed and able to survive in the outside world. In the weeks or months after birth it is fed by its mother with milk from her mammary glands.

This whole process of producing young is highly suited to land mammals. They can find shelter from enemies and choose a protected place where they can give birth in peace. Their young are born headfirst so that as soon as their heads emerge they can breathe the life-giving air around them.

But the whale is far too enormous and too far along in its adaptations to the sea to go ashore to give birth like the other sea mammals: sea lion, seal, sea otter, and walrus. The female whale, called a cow, must give birth in the water. (The male is called a bull.) In fact, the calves are born underwater, where they cannot breathe.

Again, the whales have adapted to this unusual circumstance. Whale calves are born tailfirst so that they do not need to breathe outside oxygen until their whole bodies are free of their mothers and they can swim to the surface.

*Atlantic bottlenose dolphin
with her calf*

If the calf does not surface quickly, it will drown. The mother whale knows this instinctively, and the moment the calf is born she pushes it toward the water's surface. Other whales in the area, particularly the cows, may busy themselves about her and often help get the baby to the surface.

Gestation times, or pregnancy (the baby's growth period before it is born), are shortest for the dolphins — ten or eleven months — and longest for the sperm whales — about sixteen months. Most Cetaceans give birth to one calf at a time; twins are rare.

Because the calf must surface as soon as it is born, it comes into the world with its eyes open, its senses alert, and its swimming ability well developed. For about the first year of its life, however, it stays close to its mother, swimming alongside her and feeding on her milk, gradually learning to eat fish, squid, or krill.

Soon after birth the calf begins to feed, taking its milk from one of two nipples on the mother's underbelly. Since it must keep swimming to the surface to breathe air, the calf can only feed for short periods, but it gets a good deal of nourishment. The cow is able to contract her muscles and rapidly squirt the milk into the calf's mouth.

High in fat and protein, the milk is creamy-colored and smells and tastes rather fishy. This rich milk helps the calf grow quickly. At birth, a baby blue whale may already be 25 feet long and weigh over 4,000 pounds. It is the largest baby in the world. Soon its rich diet will add pound after pound to its bulky frame, at a rate of more than 200 pounds a day. Depending on the species, the calf will feed on its mother's milk for a period of from seven months to a year or more.

During all this time the cows are immensely protective toward their young, shielding them from any roughhousing in

Dolphin calf nursing

*Female porpoise with her calf
and its "aunt" who will
stay with them for months
after the calf is born.*

the water and making sure that they do not go near any dangerous objects. The cows teach their young to obey orders. A captive dolphin was seen punishing her calf for wandering off alone by holding it against the bottom of the pool for a few seconds.

Often, calves have a "foster mother" or an "aunt" — a female who looks after them and protects them whenever their own mother has to leave them to search for food. The "aunt" fusses over the calf as if it were her own, and if the real mother dies, adopts it immediately, although usually not to the extent of letting it nurse. In the past, whalers often took advantage of the Cetaceans' protective instincts toward their young by capturing a calf first, knowing that its mother would then be an easy catch. But now, calves and nursing mothers are protected by law, although each year many are harpooned in error; unfortunately, it is virtually impossible for whalers to tell if a cow is pregnant.

Besides humans with their effective weapons, whales have few enemies, but even so their life-spans are relatively short. The newborn calf will probably not live much longer than thirty years.

ECHOLOCATION

Despite their giant size, whales have comparatively tiny eyes. The whites of their eyes are covered with a thick coating, probably as protection against the sea's saltwater. Glands in the corners of the eyes regularly secrete an oily substance that bathes and cleanses the eyes and gives further protection from the stinging water.

It is difficult to see underwater. Even just below the surface the light is murky, and in the depths of the ocean the darkness is complete. Although Cetaceans may see fairly well when they lift their heads out of the water, their vision in the sea is apparently limited. Yet sperm whales may dive thousands of feet to find food. How then, with their unremarkable eyesight, do they find it? These extraordinary mammals have their own way of finding food and avoiding dangerous objects in the sea. They use their "voices" and their ears much more than their eyes.

During World War II, fierce underwater battles took place between Allied and enemy submarines, both in the Atlantic and the Pacific oceans. The United States Navy placed hydrophones (underwater listening devices) at various points along the American coast in the hope of getting advance warning of enemy submarines approaching the mainland. One day in Spring 1942, a "warning" came over the hydrophones placed in Chesapeake Bay. To one observer, the noise sounded as though a pavement was being smashed by "a hundred pneumatic drills." The navy moved into full alert, and emergency phone calls were made to the government in Washington.

But the uproar was soon calmed. A local fisherman arrived on the scene and reported to stunned naval officials that the noises were coming, not from enemy submarines, but from fish. Some croaker fish had just returned from the open sea and had set up a full-scale underwater chorus in the bay. The naval officials were among the first to learn that the ocean depths were not the silent worlds that scientists had long believed them to be. In fact, whales, dolphins, shellfish, and ordinary fish had all been clicking, grunting, and chirping underwater since their life there began.

Since World War II, many experiments have been conducted to find out more about the sounds made by fish and by Cetaceans. Now we know that as some Cetaceans travel underwater they make short, sharp bursts of sound through their blowhole. One of the most-often heard sounds rather like a creaking door. Some of these sounds are so high-pitched that they are ultrasonic, that is, beyond the range of sound that the human ear can normally hear.

Sound travels much more effectively in water than in air

The friendly, gentle, intelligent dolphin. Note the blowhole in the center of the head and the ear slit behind the eye.

and as the sounds made by a Cetacean strike an object — perhaps a fish or a rock or a boat — they bounce back as echoes. The closer the Cetacean comes to the object, the faster the sounds bounce back. The time lag between the sounds and the returning echoes tells the Cetacean how far away the object is. This way of locating things is known as echolocation.

Unlike most mammals, whales do not have outer ear flaps. The opening through which sound passes is so tiny it is barely visible, perhaps even completely lost in some species, but the structure of the inner ear is highly sensitive. Thus, it does not matter to the whale how murky the oceans are. He is using his extraordinarily keen hearing, not his eyes, to home in on his food and avoid dangerous objects in the sea. Another unusual mammal, the bat, uses a similar form of echolocation to find its way through gloomy caverns.

During World War II, human technicians developed a working sonar. Although they knew very little about Cetaceans and echolocation at that time, they had independently invented a similar way of locating underwater objects. Sonar sends out ultrasonic sounds that return as echoes. It is used a good deal by submarines. Compared to a Cetacean's system of echolocation, however, sonar is still a relatively primitive method. Sonar, it is true, can distinguish between a pile of mud and a lump of rock, but experiments with dolphins have shown that *they* can distinguish between two different kinds of similar fish — after just one blast of sound and with their eyes blindfolded.

In one test, a female dolphin proved the immense superiority of her echolocation. With her eyes blindfolded, the dolphin had to choose between two steel balls by pressing a lever attached to the larger ball. If she chose correctly, she received a reward — a handful of mullets. The balls were by no means big; one was only two inches in diameter, and the other was just one-half inch larger. Yet, once she knew what was expected of her, the dolphin chose the larger ball twenty times in succession, without a mistake. Then the test was made even more difficult. This time the difference in the size of the balls was reduced to one-quarter inch. The researchers themselves could not see the difference and had to use measuring instruments, but the dolphin chose the larger ball nine times out of ten.

Scientists are still experimenting with some species of Cetaceans in the hope of somehow copying their extraordinary echolocation methods and thereby improving sonar. So far, they have not been able to match the animals' echolocation. Even dolphins themselves dismiss mankind's invention. Sonar signals have been transmitted to captive dolphins to see how they would react. To the scientists, the transmitted sounds seemed exactly like those made by dolphins, but the dolphins — after a moment of interest — completely ignored them.

CONVERSATIONS UNDER THE SEA

The sounds made by Cetaceans are not used for echolocation alone. Besides the creaking-door sounds the animals use when they are searching for food or navigating the seas, Cetaceans can make all sorts of other sounds; they squeal, whistle, bark, grunt, groan, or even trill like canaries. British whalers called the Beluga the "sea canary." Humpback whales actually "sing." Their "songs" last from a few minutes to half an hour and occur in complete sequences that are repeated. The songs include a number of notes and are both beautiful and moving, including a whole range of orchestral sounds.

These sounds serve for communication between Cetaceans. Whether they are traveling the oceans in herds or swimming with their mates, Cetaceans are constantly communicating with one another, and scientists have discovered just how effectively they can do this.

Communications between Cetaceans is particularly striking when one member of a group is sick and needs help. It immediately sends out a cry of distress and the others rush to assist it. We have seen that for a Cetacean to live it must breathe air regularly. But a wounded or sick toothed whale tends to sink,

A school of dolphin in
southern Pacific waters.

cutting itself off from the air supply at the water's surface. Just as the mother pushes her calf quickly to the surface the moment it is born, so other Cetaceans act in a similar way when a member of their group is sick. Dolphins have been known to support a wounded animal at the water's surface for days.

Dr. John C. Lilly, former director of a dolphin-research institute in the Virgin Islands in the Caribbean, has reported some interesting examples of first-aid communication between dolphins.

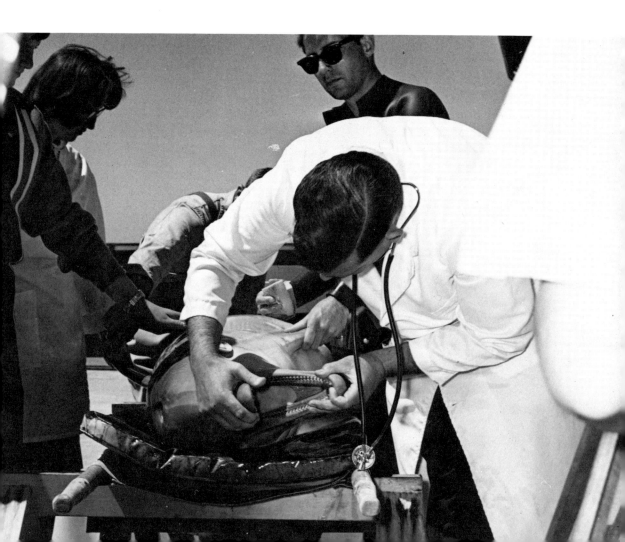

THE DIFFERENT KINDS OF WHALES

The modern species of whales, dolphins, and porpoises are divided into two groups, which have entirely different feeding habits. The largest whales, including the blue whale, belong to a group known as baleen whales. Their scientific name is *Mysticeti* (MIS-ti-SEE-tie). They get their name, baleen whales, from the sheets of horny substance called baleen that grow in their mouths. Baleen whales have a double blowhole.

The second group are known as toothed whales, or scientifically, *Odontoceti* (O-DON-to-SEE-tie). This group includes the smaller whales and one large one — the sperm whale — and the dolphins and porpoises. These whales have a single blowhole.

A veterinarian inspects the mouth of a porpoise at a Naval Missile Center Marine Biology facility. Results of this study are expected to contribute to "Man Under the Sea" programs.

THE BALEEN WHALES

For such monsters, baleen whales seem to have strange eating habits. For most of them, except humpback whales, their main food is plankton, masses of very tiny plants and animals, among them small, shrimplike creatures. Whalers have given the name "krill" to these great swarms of plankton. Krill is also eaten by other sea animals such as penguins, squid, and some fish and seabirds. Sometimes captured whales have been found to have a ton or more of krill in their stomachs.

The baleen whales are well adapted for eating their soupy meals. Instead of teeth, they have up to four hundred plates of baleen hanging from their upper jaws. Strong and flexible, the baleen is often known as whalebone, though it is not really bone at all, but keratin, the same substance as your fingernails. Baleen plates may be three or four feet long, though in the case of the Greenland right whale they may be as long as 8 feet. The inner edges of the baleen are frayed into hairy bristles, which act as strainers.

As the whale swims through the water huge quantities of krill float, or are sucked, into its open mouth. When it has a mouthful, the whale closes its jaws and pushes its heavy tongue against the bristles. This action forces the water out

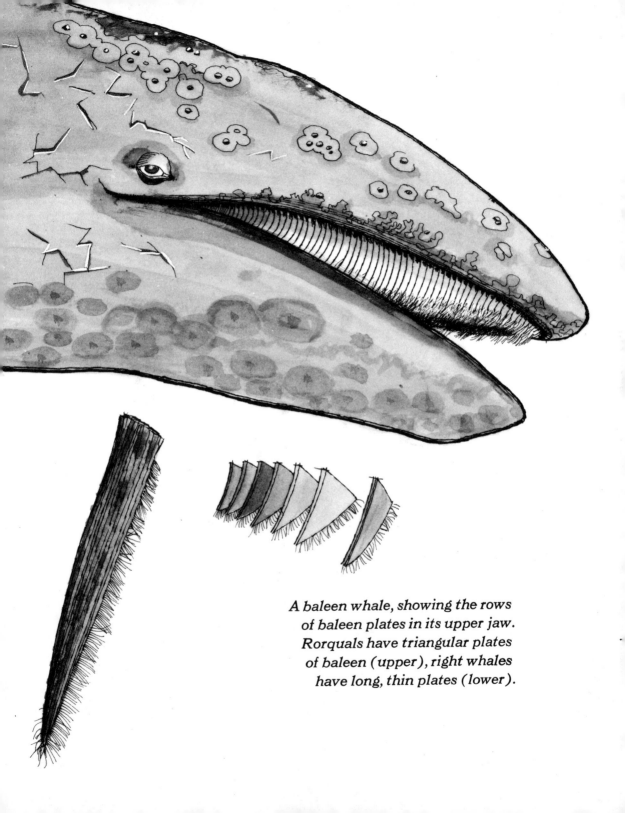

A baleen whale, showing the rows
of baleen plates in its upper jaw.
Rorquals have triangular plates
of baleen (upper), right whales
have long, thin plates (lower).

through the baleen strainers and the whale's lips into the sea, but leaves the krill stranded on the hairy bristles. After it has swallowed this mass of krill, the whale takes another mouthful.

Krill is usually found near the surface or in the upper layers of the sea, so baleen whales do not have to dive to great depths to find their food. They can dive as deep as 200 or 250 fathoms (1 fathom equals 6 feet) if they are frightened, though, and can stay underwater for a maximum of about forty minutes before they have to resurface for air.

It is no easy job to mark and keep track of whales, but since World War II thousands of them have been tagged with stainless steel darts fired from shotguns. The darts bear serial numbers, and rewards are offered for the return of these markers, with information about when and where they were found. In this way scientists have learned that many whales — and particularly the baleen whales — migrate each year to winter feeding grounds.

As winter with its violent gales comes to the Arctic and Antarctic the ice floes shift, cutting off the whales from the masses of krill on which they feed. At that time they travel vast distances, sometimes thousands of miles, to warmer waters for feeding. During the long journeys the whales may go for months without eating anything at all; by the time they arrive in warm surroundings their blubber has shrunk to a thin layer.

Here too, in warm water, the calves are born. They need warmth if they are to survive, for a calf's layer of blubber is much thinner at birth than an adult whale's.

Baleen whales are family whales. They are monogamous, taking only one mate, and are generally gentle, peaceful crea-

Looking head on at the fringed baleen plates
in the open mouth of a little piked whale.

tures who travel to and from their winter feeding grounds in large, friendly schools, with their calves and relatives. Even when the calves are old enough to have young of their own — about three years — they may still remain in a gam with their parents.

THE RIGHT WHALES

Baleen whales are subdivided into three groups. One group — the rorquals — has grooves and pleats under the chin, probably so that when these expand, the mouth can be stretched out and made bigger during feeding. The second group of baleen whales — right whales — has a highly arched jaw and a smooth chin. The third group has only one member, the California grey whale.

The three kinds of smooth-chinned whales are known as the right whales. In the very early days of whaling they were the only whales that could be captured with any success because they were slow swimmers; they did not fight back violently when attacked; and they floated after they had been killed. Most other whales sank and could not be recovered by the small boats that made up the whaling fleets. Thus the slow, gentle, unsinkable whales were the "right" ones to capture. Moreover, they furnished fine whalebone and large quantities of oil.

The largest right whale is the Greenland right whale, also known by whalers as the bowhead, because of its arched, bow-shaped head. Its head is so enormous, in fact, that it measures one third of the whale's 60-foot-long body. This whale has the longest baleen plates. Those in the middle of the upper jaw may hang down 8 feet, twice the height of a tall person. This whale has been hunted for hundreds of years, and its numbers

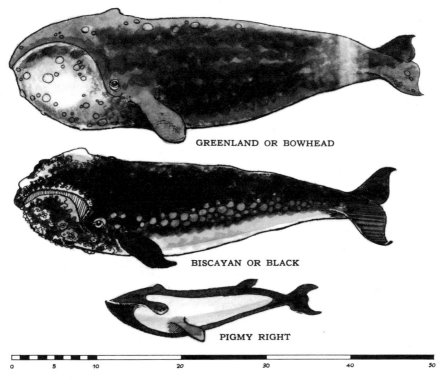

GREENLAND OR BOWHEAD

BISCAYAN OR BLACK

PIGMY RIGHT

0   5   10   20   30   40   50

The "right" whales, so called by early whalers
because they were the easiest to hunt.

are now thought to be quite small. Some bowheads are caught each year by Eskimos, but few of these whales venture away from Arctic seas.

The Biscayan, or black, whale lives only in temperate waters. It is almost as big as the Greenland right whale and is recognized by a horny lump on its snout. Whaling men call this lump a bonnet. The Biscayan whale got its name because it was originally hunted in the Bay of Biscay, off the Spanish coast, where whaling as such first began about one thousand years ago.

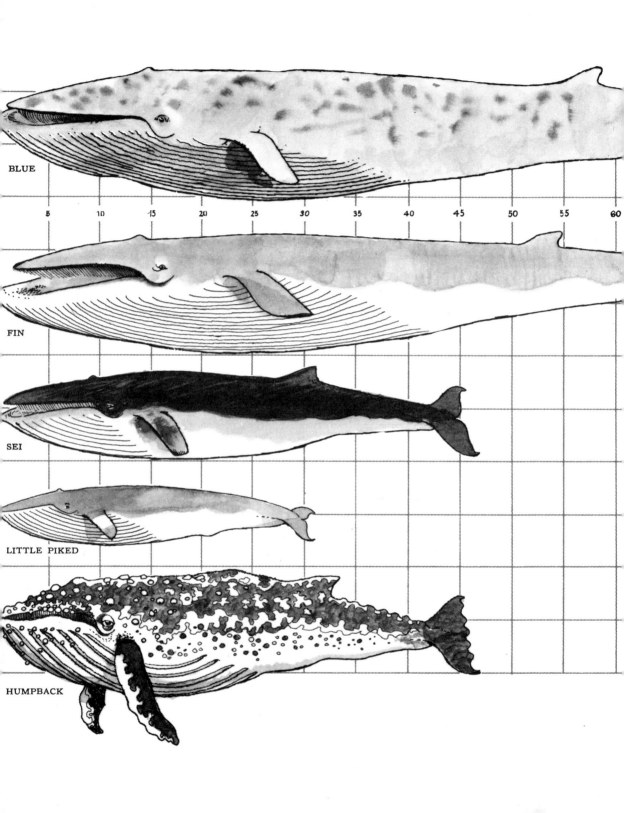

BLUE

5   10   15   20   25   30   35   40   45   50   55   60

FIN

SEI

LITTLE PIKED

HUMPBACK

The third right whale is much smaller, about 20 feet long, and is called the pigmy right whale. It is the only right whale to possess a dorsal fin and is found in the waters around Australia and South Africa.

THE RORQUALS

The whales most often sought by today's modern whaling industry, with its superior equipment, are the rorquals, those whales that were denied to early whalers because they sank when they were killed. These baleen whales have pleats under their chins, and include the blue whale and the finback whale, the two largest of the group; the sei (*say*) whale and Bryde's whale, which are similar and have been heavily hunted during the past decade; the little piked or lesser rorqual, which does not grow much more than 30 feet; and the "singing" humpback, the most acrobatic of the big whales.

The giant of the rorquals is, of course, the blue whale. This mightiest of all whales may grow to a length of 90 feet or more and weigh 150 tons. Although it cannot stay underwater the greatest length of time (it can stay submerged for perhaps 50 minutes), it is the most powerful whale. One blue whale was harpooned by a 90-foot whaling ship, but it refused to give up. It towed the ship for seven hours without stopping before it was finally killed. During the entire time, the ship's two engines were kept at full speed *in reverse.*

The blue whale has been ruthlessly hunted. At one time there were hundreds of thousands of these whales in the Antarctic. In 1966 they became nominally protected by law, but

The rorquals are baleen whales
that have been heavily hunted
in this century.

possibly it is too late: some scientists believe that the blue whale's numbers have been so drastically reduced that it may be near extinction.

The finback whale, so called because of its large dorsal fin, is often known as the greyhound of the sea because of its slender, graceful shape. The second-largest whale, the finback may grow to 70 feet and can be recognized by its distinctively shaded jaws; they are white on the right side and dark on the left. Because of the great reduction in the number of blue whales, the finbacks have become important to the whaling industry; now their numbers, too, have greatly decreased.

The humpback whale is often found in coastal waters during winter migrations. A bulky whale about 50 feet long, with large flippers that may measure as long as one-third of its body, the humpback is distinguished by the lumps on its head and flippers. Most whales dip down from the ocean's surface, but the humpback often throws itself into the air before a dive, then leaps downward into the water, its flukes remaining momentarily above the sea. Despite their bulk, humpbacks love to roll and splash in the sea, and a pod of thrashing humpbacks is a breathtaking sight.

THE "DEVIL FISH"

Another baleen whale is classified apart from the rorqual family. It is the California grey whale, which was known to old-time whaling men as the "devil fish" because of its fierce fighting whenever it sensed danger. About 45 feet in length, this creature has smashed many a small boat to pieces with its flukes.

Unlike most whales, grey whales migrate to Pacific coastal waters during the winter months, where they feed and give

*The great back of a blue whale,
a rare sight now. The blowhole
is at left, the dorsal fin at right.*

*A grey whale, its back spotted with
barnacles, on its annual southward
migration along the California coast.
It has just spouted and some of the
vapor still hangs above its blowhole.*

*A grey whale feeds by scooping up
animal life from the sea floor in its
lower jaw and then stands on its tail
to shake the food into its stomach.*

birth to their young. Coastal waters are of course dangerous to
the giant whales because of the possibility of becoming stranded, but grey whales are known to survive in shallow places.
They will swim close to shore, rubbing themselves against
rocks to get rid of the barnacles that often plague Cetaceans.

FROM CORSETS TO CRAYONS

Almost every part of the baleen whale has been put to commercial use at some time. The strong baleen, or whalebone, from
its mouth was once so valuable that the capture of one right
whale would pay for the cost of an entire whaling cruise.

At one time or another, baleen has been cut into strips and
used in ladies' corsets and in the hoops of their skirts; has been
woven to make chair seats; and has been shredded into fibers
to make sieves and brushes. Now baleen is mostly a novelty
item used mainly in the Orient for making souvenir items like
shoehorns and tea trays. Generally, plastic has taken its place.

Conservationists hope for the day when there will no longer be a market for baleen.

Baleen was not the only valuable part of these whales. Before the days of electricity, oil from the blubber and tissues was used in lamps. Today, oil from the baleen whales is extracted in large amounts and is used in many manufacturing processes. One blue whale alone used to produce more than twenty-six tons of oil. At the beginning of this century, a way of hardening oil was discovered, and it became possible to use whale oil as a base for soap, margarine, lard, crayons, candles, and even lipstick. Today, all these things can be manufactured from substitutes, making the killing of whales unnecessary.

Baleen whale meat has been eaten in many countries for centuries. More economical than beef or pork, it is high in protein and is often served raw with soy sauce in Japan. Baleen whale meat is also used to make the meat extract found in many dried and canned soups, but is most often used as an ingredient of canned pet foods.

Even the whales' jawbones were put to use in days gone by. Some were made into furniture. The reformer Martin Luther had a footstool made from a whale vertebra; it can still be seen in his house in Germany. The larger jawbones were used as rafters, gateposts, or for fencing off pastures.

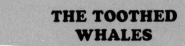

THE TOOTHED WHALES

Aside from the *Mysticeti* — the baleen whales — all the other whales, dolphins, and porpoises belong in the second group of Cetaceans known as *Odontoceti,* or toothed whales. They all have some teeth instead of baleen plates, for they do not feed on krill or strain their food as the baleen whales do. The toothed whales eat fish or squid.

Most squid are about two feet long. These lesser squid are eaten by many of the smaller toothed Cetaceans, but deep in the ocean live enormous squid whose tentacles may stretch out to 50 feet. These are the creatures that are tackled by the sperm whale.

THE SPERM WHALE

Measuring about 60 feet in length, the sperm whale is the giant of the toothed group. There are also two kinds of pigmy sperm whales that average nine feet in length. Although the bottlenosed whale may be able to stay underwater longer, the sperm whale appears to be the champion diver, plunging thousands of feet into the ocean's dark depths. With its huge jaws and teeth and with its ability to dive, the sperm whale is a superb match for the monster-sized squid that is its customary food. But although the whale is the likely winner in an underwater battle — the remains of giant squid are often found in its stomach — the sperm whale does not always escape unharmed. Captured sperm whales are often scarred around the head and jaws where the tough suckers on the ends of the squid's tentacles have cut into their skin.

Squid are not the only creatures who have reason to fear the sperm whale. Even men have been known to come out second best against this creature. In 1820, the whaling ship *Essex* was hunting whales in the Pacific. The crew had killed one sperm whale when suddenly a second one appeared. This whale was the largest the men had ever seen, and to their horror they saw that it was going to make a direct attack on the ship.

With full force the whale launched itself against the *Essex*, plunged beneath the ship, then returned again in fury. This time, the crashing impact of the whale against the ship stove in the bow. The whale made off and was never seen again, but the *Essex* was left sinking. Out of the twenty crewmen, only five survived to tell the tale.

From that time on, the sperm whale was regarded with awe and trepidation. It became the most famous whale of all. Moby Dick, in Herman Melville's classic story of that name, was a sperm whale. And if Jonah, of the Old Testament story, *was* ever swallowed by a giant "fish," the culprit was probably a sperm whale, for it is the only whale with a throat large enough to hold a man.

Sperm whales are polygamous: that is, they have more than one mate. The bulls travel with large herds of females. But when so-called summer comes to the Arctic regions, the males leave the females and calves in warm waters and make

The whaling ship Essex *and the sperm whale that rammed and sank her. The whale was an estimated 60 feet, 60 tons; the 238-ton ship was about 100 feet long.*

long journeys to the icy waters around the South Pole to feed.

Like most other Cetaceans, sperm whales love to play and frolic. Sailors have seen whole pods of them lobtailing in the water. They stand on their heads, then crash into the water with a tremendous lashing of their flukes. Sometimes an entire pod will leap out of water together, or will spout together, or will line up and swim in rows.

Since the early 1700's, when whalers began to capture them in increasing numbers, sperm whales have been the most profitable whales of all. Special reservoirs in their huge heads contain not only oil, but also a fine wax known as spermaceti, from which the whale gets its name. The whale's body temperature keeps the spermaceti in a liquid state, but when this spermaceti is removed from the whale it cools and solidifies into a white wax. At one time, this wax was made into the finest candles, and although it is not as valuable now, spermaceti is still used as a lubricant for delicate instruments, although a vegetable oil has been discovered that is good enough to replace it. The sperm oil itself is used as an agent in the dyeing of such materials as wool and linen. One sperm whale alone may produce as much as 12 tons of sperm oil.

Old-time whaling voyages were often long and monotonous. Many of the men would pass away the hours by engraving and carving the sperm whale's large teeth and jawbones. The pieces that resulted were called scrimshaw. A tooth went through many processes before it was finally sold. It was filed, ground to a smooth surface, polished, then engraved with a needle or knife. The carved lines that formed a design were filled in with soot to make them more visible, then the tooth was given a final polish. The often beautifully decorated teeth became valuable items of trade between whalers and the inhabitants of the Pacific Islands. They could be exchanged for fresh food supplies and sometimes even for brides.

But, until recent times, perhaps the sperm whale's most valuable product has been ambergris, a waxy substance used by the perfume industry to retain the odor of expensive scents. Ambergris is formed in the sperm whale's intestines and is thought to be caused by irritation from the indigestible beaks of the squid on which it feeds. Often, lumps of ambergris have been found with squid beaks embedded in them.

At one time, finding ambergris was like finding treasure. Even as late as 1912, one small whaling company was saved from bankruptcy by a timely find: it captured a sperm whale that contained a lump of ambergris weighing 1,003 pounds. This lump sold for over sixty thousand dollars. Today, ambergris might fetch about five dollars an ounce because synthetic substances have largely taken its place, and it is used only in the finest perfumes.

BEAKED WHALES

Five known genus belong to this family of toothed whales, which are usually recognized by their long, narrow snouts or "beaks." Beaked whales all have dorsal fins set well back on their bodies, much nearer to their tails than to their heads.

Although the beaked whales' main food is squid, they do not have any teeth at all in the upper jaw, and only one or two teeth set on either side of the lower jaw.

Baird's beaked whale, also called the giant bottlenose whale, is the largest of the group; it may grow to a length of 40 feet or more. But much better known to man is the bottlenose whale, once a common sight in the Atlantic as it migrated in small pods each spring and fall. There is also a bottlenose whale of the Antarctic and South Pacific. These whales grow to a length of about 30 feet and as they get older they become

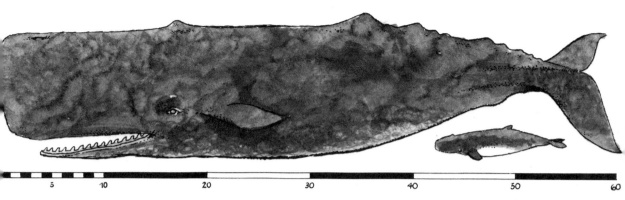

| 5 | 10 | 20 | 30 | 40 | 50 | 60 |

The blunt-headed sperm whale is the giant of the toothed whales and averages six times the length of the pigmy sperm.

Beaked whales are usually recognized by their long, narrow snouts.

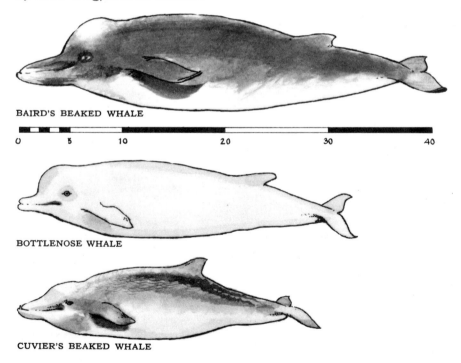

BAIRD'S BEAKED WHALE

| 0 | 5 | 10 | 20 | 30 | 40 |

BOTTLENOSE WHALE

CUVIER'S BEAKED WHALE

lighter in color — whitish-yellow. They have been captured by whalers since the nineteenth century and like other Cetaceans their numbers are getting smaller.

RIVER DOLPHINS

Most toothed whales live in the sea, but a few species — the river dolphins — inhabit fresh water. Most of these river dolphins have long, slender jaws.

Perhaps the most respected and feared is the Amazon

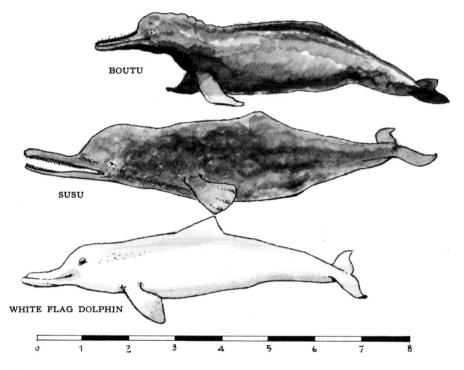

BOUTU

SUSU

WHITE FLAG DOLPHIN

0   1   2   3   4   5   6   7   8

The river dolphins are the only Cetaceans to inhabit fresh water.

River dolphin, which grows to about seven feet and feeds on fish. The people of Brazil call this creature *boutu* and never deliberately kill one, as they fear it will bring bad luck of some kind. Many of the people believe that blindness will strike anyone who uses candles made of *boutu* fat.

The *susu*, or Gangetic dolphin, lives only in the Ganges and other rivers of India. Its name comes from the noise it makes when breathing. Virtually blind, it uses its long beak to stir out fish from the muddy river bottom.

Strangest of all river dolphins is the white flag dolphin, or Chinese river dolphin, so called because its dorsal fin resembles a flag. It is found only in Lake Tungting, 600 miles up the Yangtze River in China. No one knows quite how this dolphin got there. Superstitious Chinese believe it is the ghost of a princess who drowned in the lake long ago. Pale gray and about seven feet in length, it has a very long, slender beak. Like the susu, it is almost blind.

THE UNICORN OF THE SEA

One of the toothed whale families includes the narwhal, often called "the unicorn of the sea," and the beluga. They belong to the family Dolphins in the Wider Sense.

For centuries the narwhal has been sought for its long, beautifully spiraled tusk which projects eight or nine feet from the snout of the adult male — more than half its body length. Actually, the tusk is not a tusk at all, but the Cetacean's enormously developed left tooth, which grows from the upper jaw. Sometimes, but rarely, the one other tooth, on the right side of the jaw, grows too, so that the narwhal has two tusks.

Hundreds of years ago, Greenlanders sold narwhal tusks to foreigners, claiming that they were the horns of the mythical unicorn. Many Europeans of that time believed in the magic powers of the tusks and paid fabulous sums of money for them.

Narwhals are found only in the Arctic seas. They roam the lonely miles in small herds, catching fish that they swallow whole.

THE BELUGA

The beluga has its own claim to distinction. It is the only truly white Cetacean in the world and is sometimes known as the white whale. At birth the beluga is black or dark gray, but gradually its color lightens to a yellowish-white. By the time it is about five years old it has become completely white.

Belugas are noisy creatures and often travel the Pacific and Atlantic oceans in herds of hundreds, whistling and calling to each other. The largest are 18 feet long. Belugas do not have dorsal fins.

THE KILLER WHALE

There is one black sheep in the world of Cetaceans: the killer whale. This giant of the dolphin family may grow to 30 feet and in its constant search for food has been known to attack a wide variety of ocean inhabitants: penguins, seals, squid, fish, and even other whales, dolphins, and porpoises.

Above, the white beluga whale and the narwhal, "the unicorn of the sea," are among the most distinctive of the toothed whales.

Below, the streamlined killer whale with its striking black and white markings.

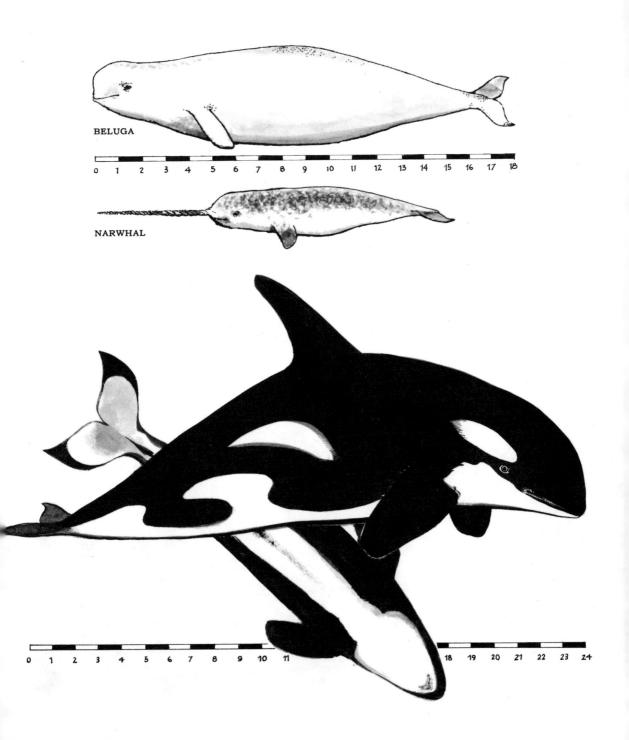

BELUGA

0 1 2 3 4 5 6 7 8 9 10 11 12 13 14 15 16 17 18

NARWHAL

0 1 2 3 4 5 6 7 8 9 10 11   18 19 20 21 22 23 24

Killer whales swim in fast, close hunting packs of up to forty or fifty individuals which may attack with cunning, circling and closing in on their victims. A pack will even attack a mammoth whale, ripping at its mouth and body with their teeth until the exhausted creature dies.

The streamlined killer whales are black with white markings and they have a distinctive dorsal fin. This fin in adult males may jut 6 feet into the air and can be seen rising out of the sea while most of the rest of the body is submerged.

Although their reputation for fierceness is second to none among sea creatures, lone killer whales have been captured and have proven to be amazingly docile in captivity. One killer whale, called Namu, was kept until its recent death at an aquarium in Seattle. Namu settled down happily. He not only allowed his trainer to scrub him regularly and feed him with fish placed directly in his open mouth, but also carried the trainer about on his back.

A killer whale leaps 22 feet out of an aquarium tank to take a mackerel from its trainer.

Two killer whales in their tank at Marineland of the Pacific.

DOLPHINS
AND PORPOISES

The time was summer in 1955. The place was Opononi Beach, a resort in New Zealand. As the bathers laughed and swam in the shallow waters a dolphin appeared among them and started to frolic alongside them. She was so friendly that people were able to pat her and play ball games with her; some even went for rides on her back. The dolphin was nicknamed Opo and her fame spread; people came from miles around, hoping to catch a glimpse of her. The government of New Zealand started to put through a law that would protect Opo, but one day in March, 1956, the dolphin was found dead. She had become stranded on some nearby rocks.

Dolphins and porpoises, the smaller members of the toothed group of whales, have always held magic for man. They have been thought of as somehow special, and even supernatural, since the earliest times. The ancient Greeks believed that dolphins were the sea chariots of the gods of Olympus, racing over the water to rescue their heroes from terrible disasters.

One of the most famous dolphin stories was told by the Roman scholar Pliny almost two thousand years ago. Not far from Naples lived a boy from a poor family, whose route to school each day took him around a large lake. In the lake lived

COMMON PORPOISE

COMMON DOLPHIN

SOUTH PACIFIC DOLPHIN

DUSKY DOLPHIN

PEALE'S DOLPHIN

SOUTHERN RIGHT WHALE DOLPHIN

DALL'S PORPOISE

Pacific bottlenose dolphins cavorting in southern California waters.

Below, a rare albino porpoise

a dolphin whom the boy named Simo. Each day on his way to school the boy would call across the lake, "Simo, Simo," until the dolphin was so accustomed to him that it would take pieces of bread from his hand. Now the boy had only to call and the dolphin would come splashing up to him. One day the boy climbed on the dolphin's back and Simo carried him across the lake to school. Each day after that the boy rode the dolphin to and from school. This went on for some years, then tragically the boy died. The dolphin returned again and again to the spot where its friend had called it, and finally it too died, doubtless, says Pliny, of "grief and sorrow."

Even today, some sailors have superstitions about dolphins. They believe that if they fall overboard, dolphins will come to their rescue and hold them up in the sea. Indeed, it is said that during World War II six American airmen who were shot down in the Pacific were towed on their raft to the safety of a small island by a friendly dolphin.

There are some fifty species, or kinds, of dolphins and porpoises and many of them confusingly have the word "whale" in their names. But all the Cetaceans talked about in this section of the book are related, whatever their names, and belong to the family with the scientific name *Delphinidae* (del-FIN-i-dee).

It is not always easy to tell the difference between a dolphin and a porpoise. Porpoises measure from about five to six feet long, and dolphins range from five feet to 30 feet, depending on the species. Both have a single crescent-shaped blowhole. The main difference is in the shape of their snouts: dolphins usually have a beaklike snout, and porpoises have blunt noses. The Romans used the Latin words *porcus pisces* for the common porpoise; these words meant "hogfish" and were given the animal because of its shape and blunt snout. From the

Latin words comes the name "porpoise." The common dolphin was called *delphinus*. From that Latin name comes the word "dolphin."

Friendly, playful creatures, these Cetaceans often travel in large, noisy schools, lashing the waves and whistling and squealing to one another. The presence of dolphins alongside a ship has long been considered a good omen and a sign of fair weather. Both animals are fast swimmers and feed on fish, swallowing them whole.

THE INTELLIGENT DOLPHINS

In recent years, dolphins have become great crowd-drawers at marinelands. If you have been to such a place, you will probably have seen the bottlenose dolphin, the most familiar one of all. Some of the displays of these animals are spectacular: they leap in formation at their trainer's command, toss balls to each other with their snouts, jump through hoops, catch fish in their open mouths, and dive deep into the tanks to retrieve objects.

Normally sociable creatures, dolphins learn tricks by a system of rewards: if they respond correctly to an act they get a fish. They learn so quickly that if they are placed in a tank with other dolphins who have already been trained, they will learn routines just by watching and copying them. It is quite likely that learning tricks helps to relieve the boredom of captivity.

Dolphins will even invent their own games. At one marineland, a dolphin was seen trying to poke an eel out of its hole between two rocks, by pulling at its tail. This method did not work, so the dolphin called for the help of a fellow tankmate, who stationed itself at the other end of the hole and tried to frighten the eel out while the first dolphin pulled. This did not work either, so the dolphin then lashed at the belly of a passing scorpion fish, killing it with one blow. The dolphin then held the fish gingerly in its mouth and ran the spines of the fish over the eel's tail. This act had the desired effect and the eel made a dash for freedom. The dolphin immediately dropped the fish, captured the wriggling eel, and began its game: throwing the eel high out of the water and catching it again and again, until finally the dolphin tired and let its plaything go.

Since the discovery of the Cetaceans' superb built-in sonar, a few experiments have been conducted to learn just how acute their intelligence is. Most of these tests have been made with dolphins, because they are fairly easy to keep in captivity. Not nearly as much is known about the pelagic porpoises; the moment they are taken out of their natural surroundings they go into shock and die. And as yet no way has been found to keep the huge baleen whales. Merely the problems of feeding them are formidable, for no marineland can provide the enormous amounts of krill on which they feed.

But dolphins have proved to be such easily trained and intelligent mammals that many scientists believe their future lies not so much in performing ever more complicated tricks for marineland audiences, but in actually *working* with humans in various fields.

The United States Navy, for instance, has been working with dolphins, sea lions, and seals for some time, training them to become assistants to aquanauts in new underwater marine laboratories. One such dolphin, a bottlenose called Tuffy, went through a rigorous period of navy training, then was sent to Sealab II some 200 feet deep in the ocean off La Jolla, California, to work with the aquanauts.

Bottlenose dolphins
performing at an aquarium.
One of the dolphins
can lift its 600
pounds fully 23 feet
out of the water.

Tuffy accepting a
fish from a U.S. Navy
Sealab II aquanaut.

One of the most frightening things that can happen to an aquanaut is getting lost outside his underwater laboratory. He may lose his guideline and suddenly find he can no longer see the reassuring lights of the lab. If this does happen, he cannot hurry upward toward the water's surface because of the fatal danger of the bends. The navy wondered if dolphins could possibly be trained to rescue aquanauts lost outside the sealabs. If they could, one of the greatest problems of underwater research would be solved.

In September 1965, the navy put Tuffy to the crucial test. Tuffy had been trained to wear a harness and to react to certain sound signals by going immediately to the source of the sound. On this particular day in September, he was swimming about in the ocean when suddenly two alarm signals went off. One came from a rescue diver, who was wearing a special sound device on his wrist; the other came from an aquanaut who, pretending he was lost, had swum away from the sealab.

Tuffy immediately went to the rescue diver, to whose call he had been trained to respond first. After the diver attached a line to Tuffy's harness, keeping one end fastened to himself, the dolphin was off again, shooting toward the second sound, which came from the "lost" aquanaut. As the dolphin swam, his end of the line unraveled and lengthened. The aquanaut, when Tuffy reached him, took the line, and Tuffy headed for the surface — just one minute and ten seconds after the operation had begun. By following the line, the "lost" man was able to find the diver to whom it was attached.

Tuffy's exciting accomplishment heralded a whole new partnership between aquanauts and sea mammals. In the future, dolphins — and perhaps sea lions, too — will probably be used for many underwater jobs. Experiments have shown that they make much more efficient messengers, for instance, than do humans. Tuffy made seven trips delivering messages to an aquanaut outside the sealab, in less time than it takes for a diver to put on all his gear. Dolphins also make speedy chariots. A dolphin can carry a man about underwater faster than a submarine can. In the future, dolphins may be used to carry heavy loads, as well; it has been found that they can easily tote hundreds of pounds of equipment about the oceans.

TALKING WITH DOLPHINS

Only a few decades ago, the very idea of actually "talking" to a dolphin would have been dismissed as the wildest fantasy. Today, although humans still cannot talk to dolphins, the idea that one day they might be able to does not seem quite so fanciful. Since the 1940's, when dolphin research began in earnest, many scientists and military and industrial groups in the United States, Russia, and Europe have been trying to find ways of communicating with dolphins. Many problems are involved.

The dolphin's brain weighs more than a human's, although of course weighty brains do not necessarily mean more intelligence. The dolphin has been found to be the most intelligent animal known to man, rating above the chimpanzee. But the fact remains that dolphins are sea creatures and humans are land creatures. If the two groups are to communicate, a great deal of complex sound equipment has to be placed in the dolphins' tank and in the scientists' laboratory. It has to be equip-

A 5,000-pound false killer whale takes a mackerel from his trainer's hand. In captivity it eats 300 pounds of squid and mackerel every day.

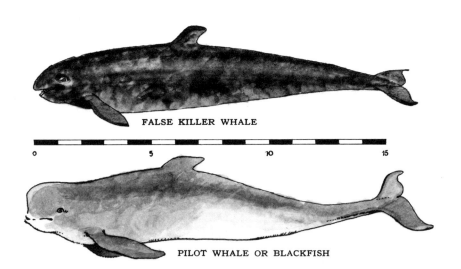

FALSE KILLER WHALE

0   5   10   15

PILOT WHALE OR BLACKFISH

ment that can "translate" to an audible level the sounds made by a dolphin when it goes above the pitch that humans can hear.

Another problem is that dolphins do not have functional vocal cords. Is it going to be possible for them to reproduce the sounds of human speech in the same way they produce sonar signals, through the blowhole? If not, will it be possible for humans to make dolphin sounds and learn to speak dolphinese? There are no full answers to these questions yet.

If people do succeed in "talking" with dolphins, the human benefits, at least, will be impressive. Dolphins already help fishermen, oceanographers, and scientists by providing new information about the oceans and navigation, and act as pickups for the space program, retrieving missiles from the oceans. And if at some future date we do find life on another planet, our knowledge of dolphin language might be a useful start in helping us to find ways of communicating with other alien forms of life.

FOLLOW-THE-LEADER

Although dolphins and porpoises have not been as extensively hunted as the larger Cetaceans, they are still captured in some parts of the world for their meat and oil. Porpoise meat was a delicacy in England during the time of Henry VIII and is eaten today by the inhabitants of some Pacific islands.

In the Solomon Islands the natives have no need for modern whaling vessels. They catch porpoises as they have done

An aquarium diver
feeds two Atlantic
bottlenose dolphins.

for centuries, by frightening them ashore. A group of canoes goes out into the Pacific and, as soon as a school is sighted, the fishermen smack large stones together underwater. The noise frightens the porpoises so much that they are easily driven into harbor, where the natives pull them ashore.

Besides eating the meat, some of the islanders make good use of the porpoises' teeth, as currency. A thousand teeth, strung into a necklace, may purchase a bride.

The natural friendliness of dolphins sometimes works against them. This instinct can lead pilot whales — or blackfish as they are often called because they are black in color — to their death.

For centuries, the fishermen and villagers of the Faroe Islands, north of Scotland, have used the natural herding instincts of these dolphins to capture them. When a large school is sighted — and sometimes there are hundreds or thousands of these blackfish, over 20 feet long, in a school — the local fishermen set out in their boats, circle round the dolphins, and guide them into the harbor by churning the water with their oars and throwing stones. The leaders of the school eventually get stranded on the shore, for there is nowhere else for them to go. Then, very often, the rest of the school plays a grim version of follow-the-leader, for they too swim ashore and become stranded. Some scientists believe that the leaders send out distress signals to the other dolphins, which go to their death in attempting rescue.

Pilot whales are found in the Pacific, Atlantic, and Indian oceans.

HUNTING
THE WHALE

In the beginning, whales came to man. Sometimes a dead whale would be found stranded on rocks or on the shore, and then whole villages would rejoice. For a few days the constant scramble for food could cease and there would be an enormous feast, with enough food for everyone. As they attacked the dead whale with their knives and spears, the villagers must have thought they had truly received a gift from the gods.

As long ago as ten thousand years, men began to go out and actively hunt the smaller species — dolphins and porpoises. Some hunters had primitive harpoons made of bone; others probably frightened the animals ashore by clashing stones together and blowing horns.

European whaling, as an industry, began in the Bay of Biscay around the tenth century. Lookouts would watch from hills above the fishing villages and as soon as they sighted whales would give a signal to the hunters. The hunters would set out in their frail boats to capture the small Biscayan right whales frisking among the churning waves. The whales were killed with harpoons, then towed ashore. Sometimes the boats never returned, having been smashed to pieces by the frightened whales.

Eventually the Biscayans, or Basques, became so efficient at killing the whales that they began to exterminate them altogether in the coastal waters around Spain and France. By the 1500's, the whalers were forced to look much farther afield for their quarry — as far as Newfoundland, off the east coast of Canada.

Other nations were soon joining the hunt for the whale. The British discovered Davis Strait, and the Dutch discovered the islands of Spitsbergen in the Arctic, off whose coasts huge numbers of right whales roamed the freezing seas. By the early 1600's, Spitsbergen had become the center of a flourishing whaling industry, with fleets of English, Dutch, Spanish, and German ships all participating. The dead whales were towed ashore and cut up, then the blubber was boiled to extract the oil.

American whaling started in much the same way it had centuries before in other parts of the world — the whales came ashore. Drift whales, as the stranded creatures were called, were highly prized when they ran aground on the New England coasts. One-third of each whale was claimed by the government, and the other two-thirds were divided between the town where the animal had been stranded and the person who had found it.

The Indians had been capturing whales from small canoes for years, but it was not until the middle of the seventeenth century that American whalers first set sail from Long Island. These first expeditions never went very far out into the Atlantic, and at night the men would return to a camp on shore. When a whale was captured, it was towed ashore and the blubber was cut up and boiled in a makeshift factory on the beach. The profits were divided among the men, and this profit-sharing system continued later, when the large whaling vessels set sail.

Capturing beluga whales
at a shore whaling station.

Whaleboats attacking sperm whales
in the nineteenth century.

Coastal whaling continued until 1712, and the small right whales were beginning to disappear when suddenly the whole industry was given a gigantic impetus. In that year, Captain Christopher Hussey and the crew of his whaling ship from Nantucket got caught far out at sea in a furious storm. They fought throughout the long night to keep their bearings and save the ship from going under. When morning came, the exhausted men looked around them and prepared to set sail for home. Suddenly a huge shape appeared in the water, and American whalers caught their first sight of a sperm whale.

Captain Hussey lifted a harpoon and threw it with all his strength. The weapon hit the whale, but did not kill it. The captain threw another harpoon. This time the sperm whale lashed at the sea, and the boat almost capsized. Extra rope was added to the line, and the whale, in its final death throes, took one last gigantic leap out of the water. Then it was still. The sperm whale was towed home to Nantucket, and deep-sea whaling was born.

About a century later, American whaling was at its peak. At that time 300-ton whaling ships circled the Pacific and Atlantic oceans, and the voyages sometimes lasted for three or four years. It was a grim life for the crewmen. The tedium of long voyages, cramped conditions, and the danger involved in actually catching the huge whales made many men desert at the first opportunity. Occasionally their share of the profits was good, but more often it was only $40 – $200 for an entire voyage.

When a pod was sighted, a cry came down from the lookout, and the action began. Whaleboats were lowered from the ship. Each boat contained a crew of six men who rowed furiously to the whales. As they drew alongside, all conversation stopped (for it is thought whales have excellent hearing) and the dangerous business of harpooning began.

The boat-steerer, as the harpooner actually was called, had the most difficult job of all. Bracing himself against the bow of the boat, he had to lift the harpoon and plunge it into the whale. When the harpoon hit the whale, the line, made of manila, would begin to uncoil and run out as the captured whale tried to escape. The line might be 1,000 feet long, and if great care had not been taken in coiling it, the rope, in running out, could catch a man's arm or leg and yank it off or pull him overboard. As the line reached its full length, it would tighten and the injured whale would carry the boat along with it, shooting over the waves. This frightening race with death was known as a Nantucket sleighride.

When the whale finally tired and surfaced, the officer in charge, called the boat-header, changed places with the boat-steerer, and the boat closed in for the final kill. The boat-header would raise a hand lance of about 12 feet and spear the whale in the lungs until it spouted blood when they would say, "His chimney is afire." Even an exhausted whale could smash a boat as it writhed in pain, and many men died in these final stages of the kill. If all went well, the whale was towed back to the ship, sometimes miles away, and lashed to its side. A wooden platform was rigged over the side so that men could get near to the whale and remove the blubber.

Even this task was dangerous. Sharks would often gather alongside the ship and wait to eat the discarded parts of the whale. If a man slipped on the blood-soaked decks, he met a horrible death in the water.

After the blubber had been removed and sliced up, it was put into huge iron kettles, which were placed over brick ovens built on the deck. The blubber was then boiled down until all the oil was removed from it. If the catch was a sperm whale, a hole was made in its head and the oil and spermaceti were ladled out into barrels. If the prey was a baleen whale, the

71

head was hoisted aboard ship and the rows of baleen were cut out of its mouth. Once all the oil and spermaceti and baleen were stored in the hold and the decks had been cleaned, the hunt began for another whale.

In the mid-1800's, whaling became a safer business, from the sailors' viewpoint, at least. A Norwegian named Svend Foyn invented a new type of harpoon fired from a gun. The tip of the harpoon was filled with gunpowder and exploded inside the whale, killing him more quickly. The new harpoon also opened up in the flesh, like an umbrella, and held up the whale's body long enough for it to be brought to the surface by a winch. This invention opened up a whole new field for whalers, for now they could more easily capture rorquals, the whales that until this time had sunk in the water the moment they were killed.

Svend Foyn did not leave his invention at that. He also designed a new type of whale-catcher ship that not only could carry his immensely heavy harpoon guns but also could go fast enough to get within firing distance of the whales. His new ship had an engine as well as sails, and had a speed of seven knots. Svend Foyn is known as the father of modern whaling.

Japan and the Soviet Union are now the world leaders in whaling, most of which takes place in the Antarctic. All United States commercial whaling has been prohibited, starting in 1971, to help protect the whales from extinction.

Modern whaling ships are a far cry from the early wooden ships. The heart of the modern fleet is the factory ship, which is equipped with radar for following the passage of whales underwater. The dead whales are hauled up ramps into the ship by steam winches and immediately a team of men sets to work. The workers, called flensers, make long, deep cuts in the whale's body, then machines strip off the blubber. After the flensers cut the blubber, the pieces are sent down a chute to the deck below, where they are minced and boiled to extract the oil. Meatcutters dismember the rest of the whale's body. The bones contain a great deal of oil, and some of these also go into the boilers. Most of the meat is frozen, but some is saved to be cooked for the crew, and some factory ships make meat extract.

Instead of factory ships, some whaling companies have shore stations that perform the same functions.

The factory ships are accompanied by smaller ships called buoy ships and catchers, equipped with echo-sounding devices to help locate and hunt down the whales. The catchers take the place of the old-time small whaleboats that were lowered from the mother ship and rowed out to capture the whales.

Sometimes helicopters are used to search for whales. Otherwise, lookouts in the catcher ships signal the alert — by calling "Blast!" — when a school is sighted. The high-speed catcher ships race to the area, then as they reach the whales they slow down and position themselves quietly. The gunner, a highly skilled marksman, fires the harpoon gun from the bow of the boat. Today's lines are not coiled in a heap on the deck of the boat, and so are less dangerous to the crew than the ropes of the early vessels were. The lines are now made of nylon, and are specially designed to absorb the strain and pressure as the whales plunge and toss in the ocean.

When the whale is dead, it is inflated through an air pipe so that it will float, and is marked with an identifying number. Before it is cast adrift, a radar buoy and flag are placed in its carcass so that it can be located and picked up later by a buoy ship and towed to the factory ship or a shore station. The buoy ships are used, too, for ferrying men and supplies to and from the factory ships.

CONSERVATION

Modern whaling companies, like the Basque whalers of long ago, have become so efficient that they are putting themselves — and the whales — out of business. There are only so many whales in the world, and the slaughter of them continues to be terrible. In 1964 alone, 63,000 whales were killed, mostly in the Antarctic. According to the New York *Times*, modern whalers have taken more whales in the last half century than were killed in the preceding four centuries.

After World War II, the International Whaling Commission was established to try and regulate the whaling business before whales became extinct altogether. Even so, some of the right whales are virtually extinct. The blue whale was not fully protected until 1966, and it is estimated that between 1,000 and 6,000 of the animals are alive, a decline in population from 200,000. Humpbacks have been similarly killed off.

Since 1946, the commission has tried to safeguard whales in various ways. The IWC sets the whaling season, defines the areas where ships may hunt for whales, and authorizes the minimum sizes, below which the different species may not be caught. It also protects nursing cows and their calves and gives complete protection to some species — the blue, the California grey, and humpback — although the regulations are followed only by the IWC member countries. Stocks of three other whales — the finback, sei, and sperm — have been reduced by more than half, but they are still hunted under yearly quotas. Conservationists fear that if the numbers of whales are reduced too far, the animals will no longer be able to find mates. Porpoises and dolphins, too, are endangered, as hundreds of thousands of them are caught and die each year in the nets of the tuna fishermen; many of them are deliberately killed by the fishermen because of the damage they do to the nets and the amount of fish they eat.

Conservationists, worried that whales will become extinct, are fighting to forbid whaling by any nation, but Japan and the Soviet Union, particularly, say they depend on whale meat as food for their people; however, much of the Soviet catch is used in pet food. Great Britain, although she no longer has a whaling fleet, still imports a number of products made of whales. Satisfactory alternatives to all whale products are available; therefore, there is no reason why all countries could not stop whaling immediately. But putting an end to whaling will be a difficult task. The whaling nations are very reluctant to give up a profitable business; for instance, whaling itself is an $80-million-a-year industry in Japan and sales of whale products there were over a billion dollars in 1970. It now seems clear that commercial whaling will result in the extinction of all whales before this century is ended, so both whales and whaling will be things of the past unless international conservation regulations are set and followed strictly.

Above, flensing a baleen whale.
Right, the flukes of a grey whale,
a species that man almost wiped out.

At the end of each whaling season a radio call goes out to all whaling ships at sea: "All whaling must cease." Perhaps, in the future, the conservationists will win and the warning will go out for the last time. Then whales and dolphins and porpoises will be able to live out their natural lives, perhaps as close partners of man, perhaps just as nature destined — following the seasons in search of food, bearing and caring for their young, and lashing the waves as they play in the oceans of the world.

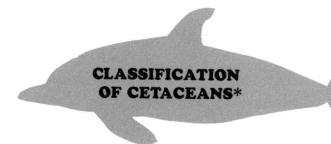

CLASSIFICATION OF CETACEANS*

BALEEN WHALES (MYSTICETI)

A. Right Whales (*Balaenidae*)
1. Greenland Right Whale
2. Biscayan Right Whale
3. Pigmy Right Whale

B. Grey Whales (*Eschrichtiidae-Rhachianectidae*)
1. Californian Grey Whale

C. Rorquals (*Balaenopteridae*)
1. Blue Whale
2. Fin Whale
3. Sei Whale
4. Bryde's Whale
5. Little Piked, Lesser Rorqual, or Minke Whale
6. Humpback Whale

TOOTHED WHALES (ODONTOCETI)

A. Sperm Whales (*Physeteridae*)
1. Sperm Whale
2. Pigmy Sperm Whale

B. Beaked Whales (*Ziphiidae*)
1. Bottlenose Whale

2. Cuvier's Whale
3. *Mesoplodon* (Sowerby's Whale)
4. *Berardius* (Baird's Beaked Whale)
5. *Tasmacetus*

C. River Dolphins (*Platanistidae*)
1. Susu or Gangetic Dolphin
2. Boutu or Amazonian Dolphin
3. La Plata Dolphin
4. Chinese River or White Flag Dolphin

D. Dolphins in the Wider Sense (*Delphinidae sensu lato*)
   a. White Whales (*Delphinapteridae*)
      1. Beluga
      2. Narwhal
   b. Porpoises (*Phocaenidae*)
      1. Common Porpoise
      2. *Phocaena spinipinnis*
      3. Finless Black Porpoise
   c. Dolphins in the stricter sense (*Delphinidae sensu stricto*)
      1. Killer Whale
      2. False Killer
      3. Irawadi Dolphin
      4. Pilot Whale
      5. Risso's Dolphin
      6. Bottlenose Dolphin
      7. Common Dolphin
      8. White-sided Dolphin
      9. *Stenella*
     10. Rough Toothed Dolphin
     11. *Cephalorhynchus*
     12. Right Whale Dolphins
     13. *Sotalia*
     14. Slender Blackfish

GLOSSARY

Ambergris – A waxy substance sometimes found in the sperm whale's intestines and formerly valuable in the making of perfumes.

Baleen – Sheets of horny substance hanging from the upper jaws of one group of whales, the *Mysticeti,* and used to strain out of the water the tiny organisms on which the animals feed.

Beaks – The long, narrow snouts found in the "beaked" whales.

Beluga – The one truly white whale.

Blackfish – The pilot whale, a member of the *Delphinidae,* or dolphins.

Blowhole – A single or double nostril placed on top of a Cetacean's head, connected directly with its lungs, and used for breathing. The blowhole has flaps that close when the animal dives.

Blubber – The insulating layer of fat found directly under the skin of Cetaceans.

Boat-header – The officer who made the final kill of a wounded whale in the old whaling days.

Boat-steerer – The harpooner in the old whaling days.

Bonnet – The horny lump on the snout of the Biscayan, or black whale.

Boutu – An Amazon River dolphin.

Bowhead – The Greenland right whale, called "bowhead" because of its arched, bow-shaped head.

Bull – A male whale.

Buoy ships – Small modern ships that locate marked floating dead whales and take them to the factory ships.

Calf – A baby whale.

Catcher ships – Small modern ships that pursue the whales and kill them.

Cetacea (see-TAY-shee-a) – The scientific name for the animal order whose members are the whales, dolphins, and porpoises.

Cetaceans (see-TAY-shuns) – The animals belonging to the scientific order *Cetacea* — the whales, the dolphins, and the porpoises.

Cow – A female whale.

Delphinidae (del-FIN-i-dee) – The scientific name for the family that includes the dolphins and porpoises.

Dolphins – Medium size and smaller members of the Cetaceans, belong to the family *Delphinidae* and known for their intelligence. They usually have a beaklike snout, a single crescent-shaped blowhole, and conical teeth.

Dorsal fin – A fin standing up on a Cetacean's back, near its tail.

Drift whales – Whales that have become stranded on shore.

Echolocation – A process used by an animal to avoid obstacles by making ultrasonic sounds that are echoed back and that thus indicate the distance and direction of objects.

Factory ships – Modern whaling ships equipped to process dead whales, extract oil, freeze meat, etc.

Flensers – Modern whaling men who strip the whales of blubber.

Flippers – The front forelimbs of the whales, dolphins, and porpoises, used by the animals for balancing, steering, and braking.

Flukes – The two lobes placed horizontally on a Cetacean's tail and used for propelling the animal through the water.

Gam – The old whaler's term for a group of whales.

Herd – Another term for a group of whales.

Humpback whale – A whale given its name because it leaps into the air before a dive, then arches downward into the water.

Killer whale – A carnivorous member of the *Delphinidae,* or dolphins.

Krill – A shrimplike crustacean. See Plankton.

Mysticeti (mis-ti-SEE-tie) – The scientific name for the baleen whales.

Narwhal – A species of toothed whale with two teeth, the left one of which grows into a long spiraled tusk. The narwhal is sometimes called the unicorn of the sea.

Odontoceti (o-*don*-to-SEE-tie) – The scientific name for the toothed whales.

Plankton – Floating masses of tiny plant and animal matter — food for some whales and other sea creatures. The whalers' name for it is *krill* because the little crustacean often makes up a large part of it.

Pod – A group of whales.

Porpoises – Smaller members of the Cetaceans, belonging to the family with the scientific name *Delphinidae,* sub-family *Phocaenidae.* Porpoises usually have blunt snouts, a single crescent-shaped blowhole, and spade-shaped teeth.

Right whales – So called because in early whaling days they were the "right" whales to catch, being slow swimmers who did not sink when killed and who furnished large quantities of oil and whalebone.

Rorquals – The group of baleen whales that have pleats, or folds, under their chins. Included in this group are the blue whale, the finback whale, the sei whale, and humpback whale.

School – A group of dolphins or porpoises; the term is not used for whales.

Scrimshaw – The engraved and decorated articles of whalebone and whale teeth fashioned by old-time whaling men to pass the time on long voyages.

Spermaceti (sperm-a-SEE-tee) – *See* Sperm whale.

Sperm whale – A toothed whale with a large head containing a reservoir of oil and a white waxy substance known as *spermaceti*.

Spout – The stream of vaporized air that rushes from a Cetacean's blowhole when it surfaces after diving.

Susu dolphin – One of the river dolphins, native to India.

White flag dolphin – A river dolphin found only in Lake Tungting, in China.

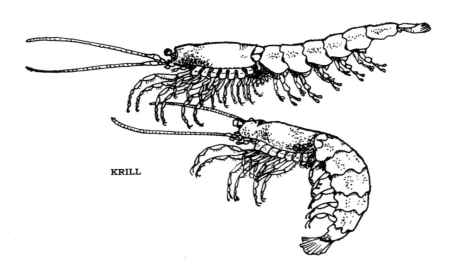

KRILL

WHERE TO SEE CETACEANS AND WHALING EXHIBITS

CALIFORNIA

Cabrillo National Monument
Point Loma, near San Diego
*(Grey whales migrate south near the
shore from December to February.)*

Marineland of the Pacific
Palos Verdes Peninsula
Palos Verdes

Sea World, Inc.
San Diego

CONNECTICUT

Mystic Seaport
Mystic

FLORIDA

Miami Seaquarium
Miami

Marineland of Florida
St. Augustine

HAWAII

Sea Life Park
Makapuu Point
Waimanalo

MASSACHUSETTS

The Kendall Whaling Museum
Sharon

Old Dartmouth Historical Society and Whaling Museum
New Bedford

The Whaling Museum
Nantucket

NEW YORK

American Museum of Natural History
New York City

New York Aquarium
Coney Island, Brooklyn

Suffolk County Whaling Museum
Sag Harbor, Long Island

Whaling Museum Society
Cold Spring Harbor, Long Island

NORTH CAROLINA

The Alfonso Whaling Museum
Beaufort

OTHER BOOKS
TO READ

Andrews, Roy Chapman. *All About Whales*. New York: Random House, 1954.

Eckert, Allan W. *In Search of a Whale*. Garden City, N.Y.: Doubleday, 1970.

Giambarba, Paul. *Whales, Whaling, and Whalecraft*. San Francisco: Scrimshaw Press, 1966.

Housby, Trevor. *The Hand of God: Whaling in the Azores*. New York: Abelard-Schuman, 1971.

Moffet, Robert L. and Martha K. Moffett. *Dolphins* (A First Book). New York: Franklin Watts, Inc., 1971.

————. *The Whale in Fact and Fiction*. New York: Harlan Quist Books, 1967.

Murphy, Robert Cushman. *A Dead Whale or a Stove Boat*. Boston: Houghton Mifflin, 1967.

Riedman, Sarah R. and Elton T. Gustafson. *Home is the Sea: for Whales*. New York: Abelard-Schuman, 1966.

Scheffer, Victor B. *Little Calf*. New York: Charles Scribner's Sons, 1970.

Shapiro, Irwin. *The Story of Yankee Whaling*. New York: American Heritage, 1959.

Songs of the Humpback Whale (LP record). New York: Capitol Records, 1970.

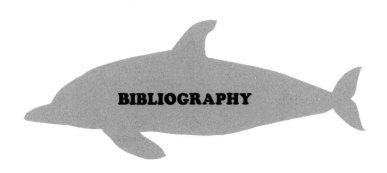

BIBLIOGRAPHY

Alpers, Antony. *Dolphins.* London: John Murray, 1960 and 1963.

Bennett, A. G. *Whaling in the Antarctic.* Edinburgh and London: William Blackwood & Sons, Ltd., 1931.

Blond, Georges, trans. by James Cleugh. *The Great Whale Game.* London: Weidenfeld & Nicholson, 1954.

Jenkins, James T. *Whales and Modern Whaling.* London: H. F. & G. Witherby, 1932.

Harrison, Richard J. and Judith E. King. *Marine Mammals.* London: Hutchinson & Co. Ltd., 1965.

Lilly, John C. *Man and Dolphin.* Garden City, N.Y.: Doubleday, 1961.

Matthews, Leonard Harrison, Ed. *The Whale.* London: George Allen & Unwin, 1968.

Robertson, R. B. *Of Whales and Men.* London: Macmillan & Co., Ltd., 1956.

Scheffer, Victor B. *The Year of the Whale.* New York: Charles Scribner's Sons, 1969.

Slijper, E. J. *Whales.* London: Hutchinson & Co., Ltd., 1962.

Stenuit, Robert, trans. by Catherine Osborne. *The Dolphin, Cousin to Man.* London: J. M. Dent & Sons, Ltd., 1968.

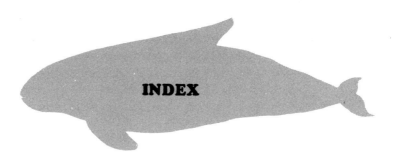

INDEX

ABOUT THE AUTHORS

Helen Hoke's first job was with her father's country newspaper in a small Pennsylvania town. Since then she has been a teacher, a book-shop manager, an editor, and a prolific writer of books for children and adults. WHALES is her seventieth book.

She is married to publisher Franklin Watts. They live in London, England where she continues to write and edit from a house with a lovely roof garden.

Valerie Pitt was born and educated in England and received a diploma in journalism from London Polytechnic. She has been a reporter and writer for several English newspapers and magazines. At present she lives in London where she writes a book review column for an English monthly. She is the author of a number of children's books.